DECLARE!

31 Day Devotional

LIFE OUTREACH INTERNATIONAL

Declare!: 31 Day Devotional

Copyright © 2023 Life Outreach International

All rights reserved. No part of this book may be reproduced or transmitted in any form or by any means, electronic or mechanical, including photocopying, recording, or by any information storage and retrieval system, without permission in writing from the publisher.

Scripture quotations marked AMP are from the Amplified® Bible (AMP), Copyright © 2015 by The Lockman Foundation. Used by permission. lockman.org

Scripture quotations marked ESV are from The ESV® Bible (The Holy Bible, English Standard Version®), copyright © 2001 by Crossway, a publishing ministry of Good News Publishers. Used by permission. All rights reserved.

Scripture quotations marked KJV are taken from the King James Version®. Public Domain.

Scripture quotations marked NASB are taken from the (NASB®) New American Standard Bible®, Copyright © 1960, 1971, 1977, 1995, 2020 by The Lockman Foundation. Used by permission. All rights reserved. lockman.org

Scripture quotations marked NIV are taken from the Holy Bible, New International Version®, NIV®. Copyright © 1973, 1978, 1984, 2011 by Biblica, Inc.™ Used by permission of Zondervan. All rights reserved worldwide. www.zondervan.com The "NIV" and "New International Version" are trademarks registered in the United States Patent and Trademark Office by Biblica, Inc.™

Scripture quotations marked NKJV are taken from the New King James Version®. Copyright © 1982 by Thomas Nelson. Used by permission. All rights reserved.

Scripture quotations marked NLT are taken from the *Holy Bible*, New Living Translation, copyright © 1996, 2004, 2015 by Tyndale House Foundation. Used by permission of Tyndale House Publishers, Carol Stream, Illinois 60188. All rights reserved.

ISBN: 978-1-951701-58-1

Assembled and Produced for Life Outreach International by
Breakfast for Seven
breakfastforseven.com

Printed in the United States of America.

CONTENTS

ADONAI *(Sovereign Lord)* 8
ELOHIM *(Creator)* 12
ELOHIM CHAYIM *(Living God)* 16
EL CHANNUN *(Gracious God)* 20
EL DE'OT *(God of Knowledge)* 24
EL ECHAD *(The One God)* 28
EL ELYON *(Most High God)* 32
EL EMET *(God of Truth)* 36
EL GIBHOR *(Mighty God)* 40
EL HANNORA *(Awesome God)* 44
EL OLAM *(Everlasting God)* 48
EL ROI *(The God Who Sees Me)* 52
EL SALI *(God My Rock)* 56
EL SHADDAI *(Almighty)* 60
IMMANUEL *(God With Us)* 64

JEHOVAH ELOHAY *(The Lord My God)*..68

JEHOVAH EZER *(The Lord Our Helper)*..72

JEHOVAH GMOLAH *(The Lord Who Rewards)*......................................76

JEHOVAH HOSEENU *(The Lord Our Maker)*..80

JEHOVAH JIREH *(The Lord Will Provide)*...84

JEHOVAH MAKKEH *(The Lord Who Molds Me)*....................................88

JEHOVAH MEKODDISHKEM *(The Lord Who Sanctifies You)*.............92

JEHOVAH NISSI *(The Lord My Banner)*..96

JEHOVAH RAAH *(The Lord My Shepherd)*...100

JEHOVAH RAPHA *(The Lord Who Heals)*...104

JEHOVAH SABAOTH *(The Lord of Hosts)*..108

JEHOVAH SHALOM *(The Lord is Peace)*..112

JEHOVAH SHAMMAH *(The Lord is There)*..116

JEHOVAH TSIDKENU *(The Lord Our Righteousness)*........................120

QANNA *(Jealous)*...124

YAHWEH *(I Am)*..128

I will declare your name to my people; in the assembly I will praise you.

— **PSALM 22:22**

As Christians, we are well aware of God's name from the first scripture in Genesis: *"In the beginning God created the heavens and the earth"* (Genesis 1:1). Immediately, He establishes Himself as the Creator of all the wonder of this world and the heavens above. The Old Testament continues to reveal God and His ways as we read of His encounters with Abraham, Moses, the prophets and the people of Israel through their history.

But the Bible also provides a much deeper, more intimate look at the characteristics of God, as the names of God are revealed in Scripture.

In this devotional, you will find 31 names of God that give insight into the loving and righteous character of God and speak encouragement to your soul. Many of us know God is referenced as ADONAI, or *Sovereign Lord*, or EL SHADDAI, *Almighty*, or IMMANUEL,

God with us. Our prayer for you is that as you read through this 31-day devotional, you will discover the personal, intimate and loving Heavenly Father who desires to be in your life and a new, or renewed, sense of *"God **with me**."*

Betty and I can testify to the enduring provision of God and the growing personal relationship with Him in our home, marriage and 60 years of ministry.

He has revealed Himself as. . .

JEHOVAH ELOHAY, *The Lord my God.*
JEHOVAH RAAH, *The Lord my Shepherd.*
JEHOVAH NISSI, *The Lord my Banner.*

And certainly, we have seen God's character as JEHOVAH JIREH, *The Lord Will Provide,* helping meet spiritual, emotional and financial needs. As you grow in your knowledge of God and His ways, you understand more fully His desire to walk and talk with you, just as

He did with Adam in the garden of Eden. And as you read through the many names of God, I believe you will join with the psalmist who wrote, *"I will declare your name to my people; in the assembly I will praise you"* (Psalm 22:22). The names of God reveal the character of God and give comfort, encouragement and inspiration in your walk with Him.

The readings in this devotional will only take a few minutes of your time each day but can lead to years of a deeper and more loving relationship with your Father in heaven. Each day you will find another name from Scripture followed by a devotional writing. This is your time to reflect, pray, give thanks, and even make personal notes for a new insight into the character of God.

God bless you as you read and meditate on the names and character of our God.

James & Betty Robison

James and Betty Robison

DAY 1

ADONAI

(Sovereign Lord)

After this, the word of the L ORD came to Abram in a vision: "Do not be afraid, Abram. I am your shield, your very great reward." But Abram said, "Sovereign L ORD, what can you give me since I remain childless and the one who will inherit my estate is Eliezer of Damascus?" And Abram said, "You have given me no children; so a servant in my household will be my heir." Then the word of the L ORD came to him: "This man will not be your heir, but a son who is your own flesh and blood will be your heir." He took him outside and said, "Look up at the sky and count the stars — if indeed you can count them." Then he said to him, "So shall your offspring be."

GENESIS 15:1-5

DAY 1

"Sovereign Lord" — Adonai — "what can You give me . . . ?" Oh, Abram! He knows that God is all-powerful, infinitely wonderful, Master of his life and supreme Ruler over all the Earth. And yet he cannot see past his own circumstances, past what the world had given him, in order to rest in the promise that Adonai had made: that Abram's descendants, the children of his seed, would one day fill the Earth.

God reminds Abram to turn his eyes away from his circumstances and on to God's Sovereignty: "Look up at the sky and count the stars . . ." Who made those stars? Who rules those stars? Adonai Himself. If God can number the stars, certainly He can number Abram's children!

O lord, our Lord, how majestic and glorious and excellent is Your name in all the earth! You have displayed Your splendor above the heavens (Psalm 8:1 AMP).

SOVEREIGN LORD

How have you seen God move as the Sovereign Lord?

_____

_____

_____

_____

What is the Lord saying to you today about His name as ADONAI?

_____

_____

_____

_____

In the beginning God (Elohim) created [by forming from nothing] the heavens and the earth. The earth was formless and void or a waste and emptiness, and darkness was upon the face of the deep [primeval ocean that covered the unformed earth]. The Spirit of God was moving (hovering, brooding) over the face of the waters. And God said, "Let there be light"; and there was light. God saw that the light was good (pleasing, useful) and He affirmed and sustained it; and God separated the light [distinguishing it] from the darkness. And God called the light day, and the darkness He called night. And there was evening and there was morning, one day.

GENESIS 1:1-5 AMP

DAY 2

ELOHIM

The very first thing that Scripture reveals about God is that He is the Creator. *In the beginning God (Elohim) . . .* Before time began there was God, and when only God existed, Elohim created all things . . . the heavens, the Earth; light, darkness; land, water; grass, trees; birds, fish; animals; humans. Elohim is the all-powerful Creator of the universe.

Genesis means "beginning." Elohim is the Creator of beginnings and new beginnings. He created cycles and seasons, times of barrenness, and times of new life. His Creation began with Adam and Eve in the garden of Eden, and it began again with Noah and the flood, and yet again with His own Son, Jesus. Elohim gave His servant Job an abundance of blessings, and after he lost everything, God restored everything to Job in double.

God told Jeremiah that He knew him in his mother's womb and predestined a purpose for his life. As the Ultimate Creator, Elohim is constantly in the process of creating and recreating all things according to His divine plan.

The heavens declare the glory of God; the skies proclaim the work of his hands (**Psalm 19:1**).

CREATOR

How have you seen God move as the Creator?

_____

_____

_____

_____

What is the Lord saying to you today about His name as ELOHIM?

_____

_____

_____

_____

As the deer pants for the water brooks, so pants my soul for You, O God.

My soul thirsts for God, for the living God. When shall I come and appear before God?

PSALM 42:1-2 NKJV

DAY 3

During World War II, a member of the Army Air Corps, Louis Zamperini, spent 47 days adrift at sea on a raft after his warplane went down. Those 47 days were filled with sharks, being shot at by Japanese planes, and only the occasional rainwater to drink. After 47 days in the scorching heat, Zamperini longed for water.

Zamperini's rescue landed him in a Japanese prison camp, where he would be physically and psychologically tortured for more than two years. When the war ended and he was released, Zamperini discovered in himself a different kind of thirst — a thirst he attempted to satisfy with alcohol, but a thirst that he could not seem to satisfy.

It wasn't until 1949, when Zamperini's wife convinced him to go to a Billy Graham crusade, that he discovered what his soul was really thirsting for: Elohim Chayim — the Living God.

Zamperini gave his life to Christ and was never the same. He could see all the places where the Living God had been alive and active and with him through his trials, and the Lord's presence allowed him to not only overcome alcoholism, but to also go back to Japan to forgive his captors. For the rest of his life, until his death in 2014 at the age of 97, Zamperini was an inspirational writer and speaker who taught others about the One who will satisfy the thirst within: Elohim Chayim.

LIVING GOD

How have you seen God move as the Living God?

_____

_____

_____

_____

What is the Lord saying to you today about His name as ELOHIM CHAYIM?

_____

_____

_____

_____

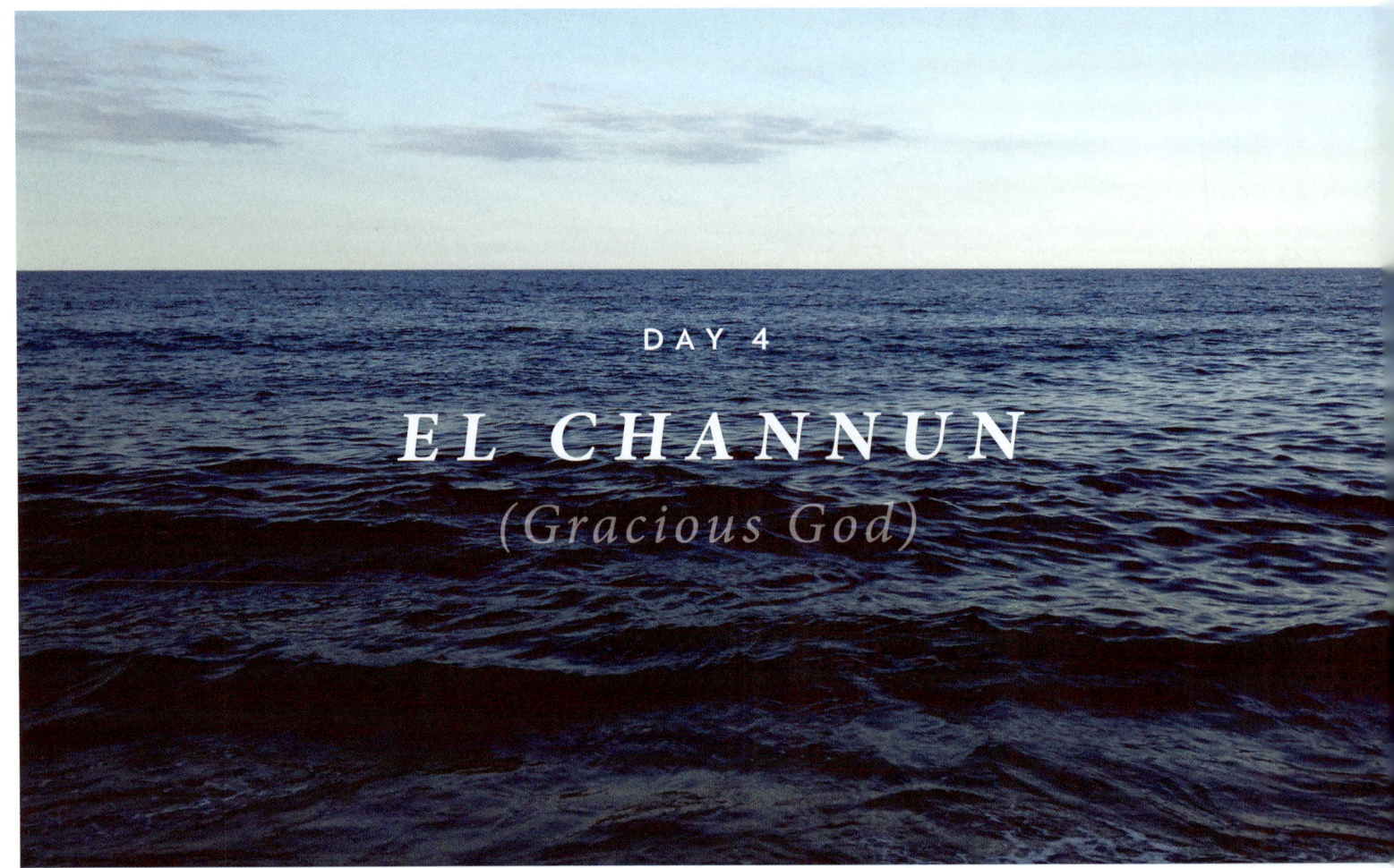

But it displeased Jonah exceedingly, and he was angry. And he prayed to the Lord and said, "O Lord, is not this what I said when I was yet in my country? That is why I made haste to flee to Tarshish; for I knew that you are a gracious God and merciful, slow to anger and abounding in steadfast love, and relenting from disaster."

JONAH 4:1-2 ESV

DAY 4

EL CHANNUN

Jonah is well-known for disobeying God and ending up in the belly of a big fish for three days. But Jonah's story teaches us more than the consequences of disobedience; it teaches us about our tendency toward judgment and God's propensity for grace.

In the first chapter of Jonah, God tells Jonah to go to Nineveh and tell the people that God will soon overthrow them for their evil deeds. Jonah flees in the opposite direction, which is how he ends up in the belly of the fish. In chapter three, God again tells Jonah to go to Nineveh, and this time Jonah obeys.

He tells the people that God's judgment is about to come upon them, and the people respond by fasting and praying to the Lord. God sees their repentance and forgives them.

Jonah prayed to God, "I knew You were El Channun — Gracious God — which is why I ran in the opposite direction in the first place!" Jonah couldn't hide his anger and indignation. The Ninevites deserved punishment. At the Lord's command, Jonah told them they would receive punishment. And here God was letting them off the hook!

Jonah's argument is almost comical: *Why do You have to be gracious and merciful? Why do You have to be slow to anger and abounding in steadfast love? Why can't You just bring disaster upon those who deserve it?!*

El Channun doesn't punish Nineveh, and He doesn't punish Jonah for his temper tantrum either. Graciously, He reminds Jonah who made the trees, the sun, the wind, and the people, and therefore who has the right to judge and the right to show grace.

GRACIOUS GOD

How have you seen God move as a Gracious God?

_____

_____

_____

_____

What is the Lord saying to you today about His name as EL CHANNUN?

_____

_____

_____

_____

"Talk no more so very proudly;

Let no arrogance come from your mouth,

For the Lord is the God of knowledge;

And by Him actions are weighed."

1 SAMUEL 2:3 NKJV

DAY 5

EL DE'OT

In Hannah's prayer, she calls God "El De'ot" — the God of knowledge. He is omniscient — all-knowing and all-seeing. Hannah knows this about God because He has just heard her prayer, seen her heart and given her the child she longed for. In her prayer to God for a child, she vowed to dedicate the boy — Samuel — to the Lord's service. And because the Lord could see her heart, He knew that she would keep her promise. And so she did.

Hannah is not the only person in Scripture who recognizes God as El De'ot. In Psalm 139, David makes the same proclamation:

> *O Lord, You have searched me and known me.*
> *You know my sitting down and my rising up;*
> *You understand my thought afar off.*
> *You comprehend my path and my lying down,*
> *And are acquainted with all my ways.*
> *For there is not a word on my tongue,*
> *But behold, O Lord, You know it altogether.*
> *You have hedged me behind and before,*
> *And laid Your hand upon me.*
> *Such knowledge is too wonderful for me;*
> *It is high, I cannot attain it.*
> (vv. 1–6 NKJV)

David recognizes that God has a knowledge that is far above even his as the king of Israel. God knows our actions; God knows our thoughts; God knows every word that we speak. David goes so far as to say that there is nowhere we can hide from God that He doesn't know where we are.

There is peace in believing in El De'ot, because we have no secrets from Him. And no matter what thoughts, words or actions that He sees, His love for us never falters.

GOD OF KNOWLEDGE

How have you seen God move as the God of Knowledge?

_____

_____

_____

_____

What is the Lord saying to you today about His name as EL DE'OT?

_____

_____

_____

_____

DAY 6

EL ECHAD

(The One God)

Have we not all one Father?

Has not one God created us?

Why do we deal treacherously with one another

By profaning the covenant of the fathers?

MALACHI 2:10 NKJV

DAY 6

EL ECHAD

The entire Old Testament can be looked at as a battle for the title of El Echad — the One God. Monotheism (the belief in one god) was not common practice in those days, and God repeatedly tried to keep Israel pure — away from the polytheistic practices of the other nations — by telling them not to intermarry, instructing them to completely destroy other nations and their idols, and performing miraculous acts to prove He was the One true God.

In 1 Kings 18, Elijah puts one of the false gods — Baal — to the test against El Echad — the One God. Elijah tells Baal's prophets to prepare a sacrifice to their god, and he will prepare a sacrifice to his God, and whichever god answers by fire is El Echad — the One true God.

The prophets of Baal call on their god to bring fire, but to no avail. Elijah, however, drenches his offering with water, bucket after bucket of water, and then finally calls on God to bring fire, to prove He is God:

> *Then the fire of the LORD fell and consumed the burnt sacrifice, and the wood and the stones and the dust, and it licked up the water that was in the trench. Now when all the people saw it, they fell on their faces; and they said, "The LORD, He is God! The LORD, He is God!"* (1 Kings 18:38–39 NKJV)

"Hear, O Israel: The LORD our God, the LORD is one! You shall love the LORD your God with all your heart, with all your soul, and with all your strength" **(Deuteronomy 6:4–5 NKJV).**

THE ONE GOD

How have you seen God move as the One God?

_____

_____

_____

_____

What is the Lord saying to you today about His name as EL ECHAD?

_____

_____

_____

_____

DAY 7

EL ELYON

(Most High God)

At the end of the time I, Nebuchadnezzar, lifted my eyes to heaven, and my understanding returned to me; and I blessed the Most High and praised and honored Him who lives forever.

DANIEL 4:34 NKJV

DAY 7

EL ELYON

Satan made the mistake of thinking that he could exalt himself above God (Isaiah 14:12–15). Many kings and presidents and CEOs, from biblical times to the present, have also made the mistake of thinking that they hold ultimate power. Nebuchadnezzar was one of those kings.

His story is found in Daniel chapters 1–4. Nebuchadnezzar was king of Babylon, appointed by God to that position: *"You, O king, are a king of kings. For the God of heaven has given you a kingdom, power, strength, and glory"* (Daniel 2:37 NKJV). But Nebuchadnezzar lost sight of who was really in charge. The power, as they say, "went to his head."

In Daniel chapter 3, Nebuchadnezzar makes an idol out of gold and instructs his entire kingdom to worship the statue or else be thrown into the fiery furnace. Three men refuse to worship the idol, declaring that even if God chooses not to rescue them, they will not bow down to another god.

As promised, Nebuchadnezzar ties them up and throws them into the fiery furnace. And he can't believe what he sees: the men, unbound and unscathed, walking around the furnace (v. 25).

> *Then Nebuchadnezzar went near the mouth of the burning fiery furnace and spoke, saying, "Shadrach, Meshach, and Abed-Nego, servants of the Most High God, come out, and come here." Then Shadrach, Meshach, and Abed-Nego came from the midst of the fire.* (v. 26 NKJV)

What does Nebuchadnezzar call the One who saved the men from burning up? "The Most High God." Nebuchadnezzar may have been king of Babylon, but he knew he couldn't take credit for this miracle. There is only One who is the Most High — El Elyon.

MOST HIGH GOD

How have you seen God move as the Most High God?

_____

_____

_____

_____

What is the Lord saying to you today about His name as EL ELYON?

_____

_____

_____

_____

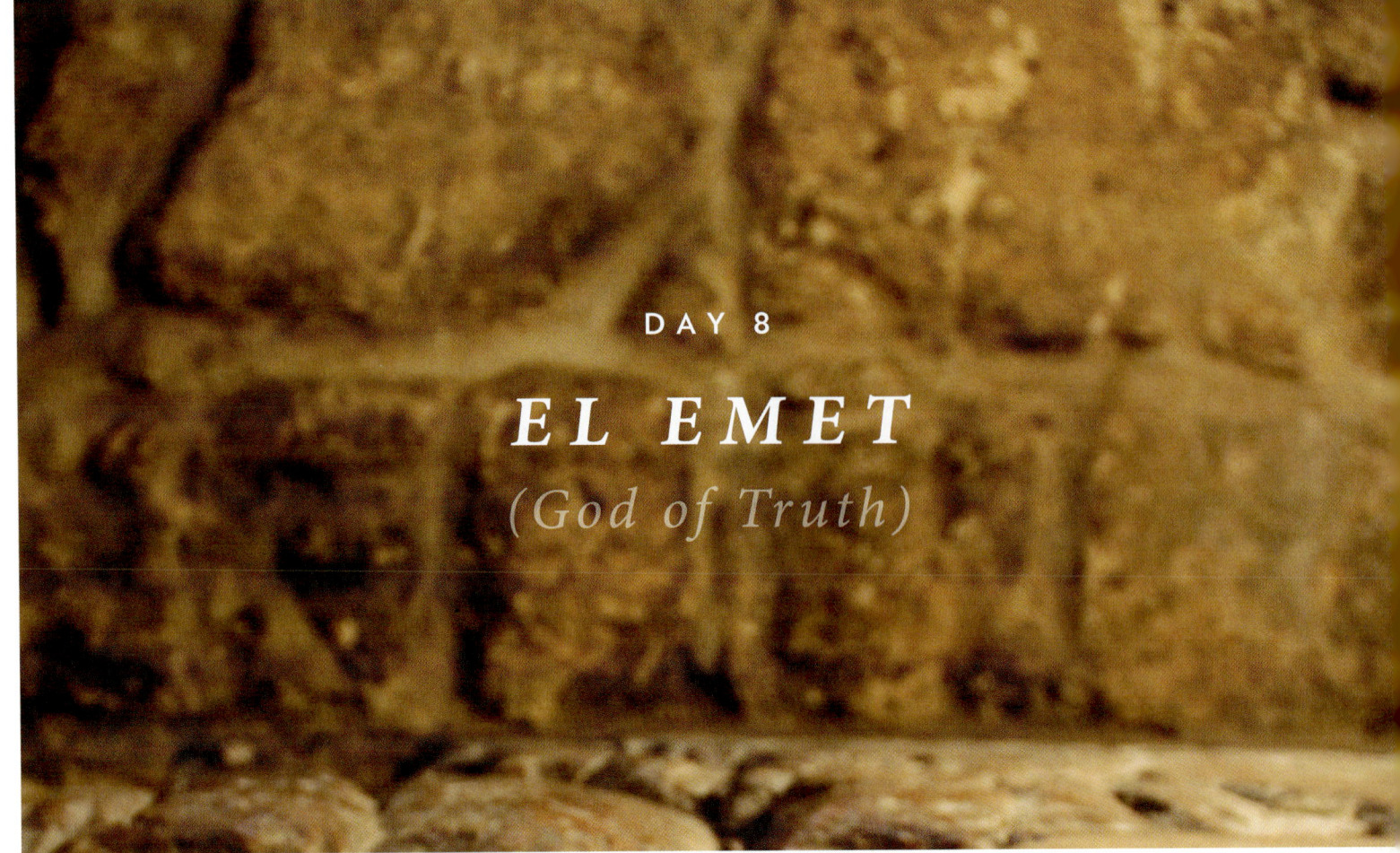

For You are my rock and my fortress;

Therefore, for Your name's sake,

Lead me and guide me.

Pull me out of the net which they have secretly laid for me,

For You are my strength.

Into Your hand I commit my spirit;

You have redeemed me, O Lord God of truth.

PSALM 31:3–5 NKJV

DAY 8

EL EMET

God is the God of Truth — El Emet. He is firm, faithful and reliable. In Psalm 31, David cries out to God in gratitude for being everything that his adversaries are not: When people are unreliable, the Lord is reliable. When others turn against him and try to secretly trap him, David can trust God to be faithful. When his foes tell lies and falsehoods, El Emet stands firm as the God of Truth.

We have all been let down at one time or another. We speak to someone in confidence, only to find out later that they've shared our private conversation with others. We are promised a promotion that is given to someone else. We make vows that aren't kept. And the opposite is also true: We, too, fall short. We have been unfaithful and unreliable and soft in our convictions.

But take heart! As David declares in Psalm 31:5, *You have redeemed me, O Lord God of truth* (NKJV). Even when we fail, even when others fail us, God redeems those failures because He is the God of Truth, who is always faithful.

Jesus said to him, "I am the [only] Way [to God] and the [real] Truth and the [real] Life; no one comes to the Father but through Me" **(John 14:6 AMP).**

GOD OF TRUTH

How have you seen God move as the God of Truth?

_____

_____

_____

_____

What is the Lord saying to you today about His name as EL EMET?

_____

_____

_____

_____

DAY 9

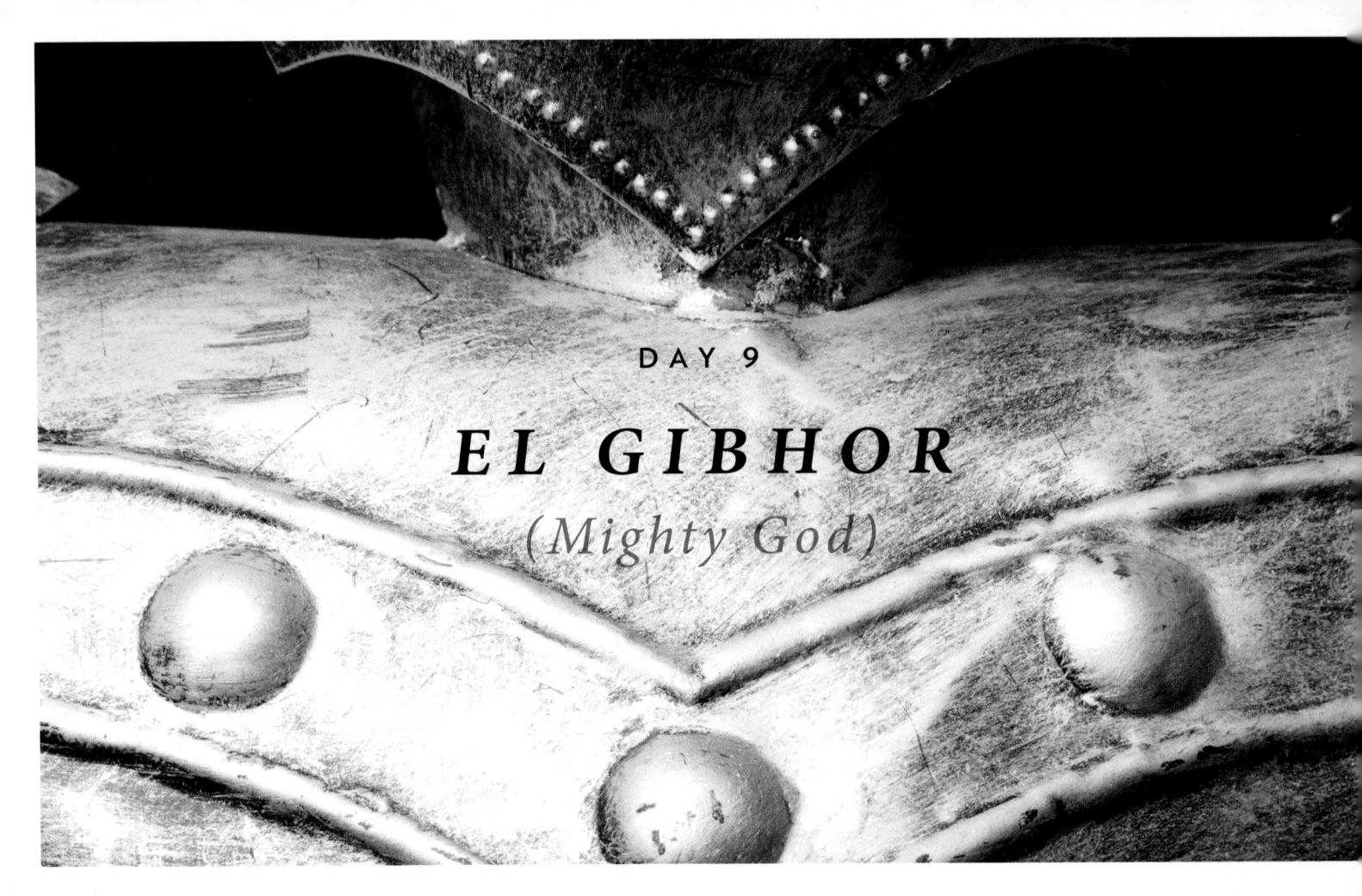

EL GIBHOR
(Mighty God)

"You show lovingkindness to thousands, and repay the iniquity of the fathers into the bosom of their children after them — the Great, the Mighty God, whose name is the Lord of hosts. You are great in counsel and mighty in work, for Your eyes are open to all the ways of the sons of men, to give everyone according to his ways and according to the fruit of his doings."

JEREMIAH 32:18–19 NKJV

DAY 9

This passage in Scripture reminds us that nothing is too difficult for El Gibhor — Mighty God (v. 18). He made the heavens and the Earth (v. 17). He performed signs and wonders (v. 20). He brought the people out of Egypt into a land flowing with milk and honey (vv. 21–22). He decides which army will win each battle (v. 24). And He decides how each person shall be rewarded or punished for their deeds (vv. 18–19).

El Gibhor is a powerful and mighty warrior, and yet this passage shows Him as just, and a rewarder for those who diligently seek Him (Hebrews 11:6).

How does one reconcile a compassionate God who shows lovingkindness with a mighty warrior? By remembering that man is not God's enemy, but evil. Therefore "the battle is the LORD's" in the battle against evil (1 Samuel 17:47). It is in that battle that God will rule with a rod of iron in order to destroy His enemies (Revelation 19:15).

For unto us a Child is born, unto us a Son is given; and the government will be upon His shoulder. And His name will be called Wonderful, Counselor, Mighty God, Everlasting Father, Prince of Peace **(Isaiah 9:6 NKJV).**

MIGHTY GOD

How have you seen God move as a Mighty God?

___

___

___

___

What is the Lord saying to you today about His name as EL GIBHOR?

___

___

___

___

![DAY 10: EL HANNORA (Awesome God)]

DAY 10

EL HANNORA

(Awesome God)

"Now therefore, our God,

The great, the mighty, and awesome God,

Who keeps covenant and mercy:

Do not let all the trouble seem small before You

That has come upon us,

Our kings and our princes,

Our priests and our prophets,

Our fathers and on all Your people,

From the days of the kings of Assyria until this day."

NEHEMIAH 9:32 NKJV

DAY 10

"Awesome" is a word we use far too lightly. When a basketball player makes a three-point shot we cry, "Awesome shot!" When our children come to us with an "A" on a homework assignment we declare, "Awesome job!" When a friend invites us out for coffee we say, "Sounds awesome!"

But Scripture tells us that we have an Awesome God — El Hannora — so we know that "Awesome" is a word that should carry more weight than a slam dunk, a good grade, or an exciting opportunity.

"Awesome" actually means "to inspire great admiration or fear." Throughout the Scriptures we are told to "fear God":

> *The [reverent] fear of the LORD [that is, worshiping Him and regarding Him as truly awesome] is the instruction for wisdom [its starting point and its essence]; and before honor comes humility.* (Proverbs 15:33 AMP)

To fear the Lord is to give Him a place of authority in your life, to humble yourself and to give God His proper honor — to regard Him as "truly awesome." To fear God and recognize His awesomeness is the beginning of knowing and understanding who God is and the role He plays in your life. Our God is El Hannora — an Awesome God!

"... *The* LORD *your God, the great and awesome God, is among you*" (**Deuteronomy 7:21 NKJV**).

AWESOME GOD

How have you seen God move as an Awesome God?

_____

_____

_____

_____

What is the Lord saying to you today about His name as EL HANNORA?

_____

_____

_____

_____

DAY 11

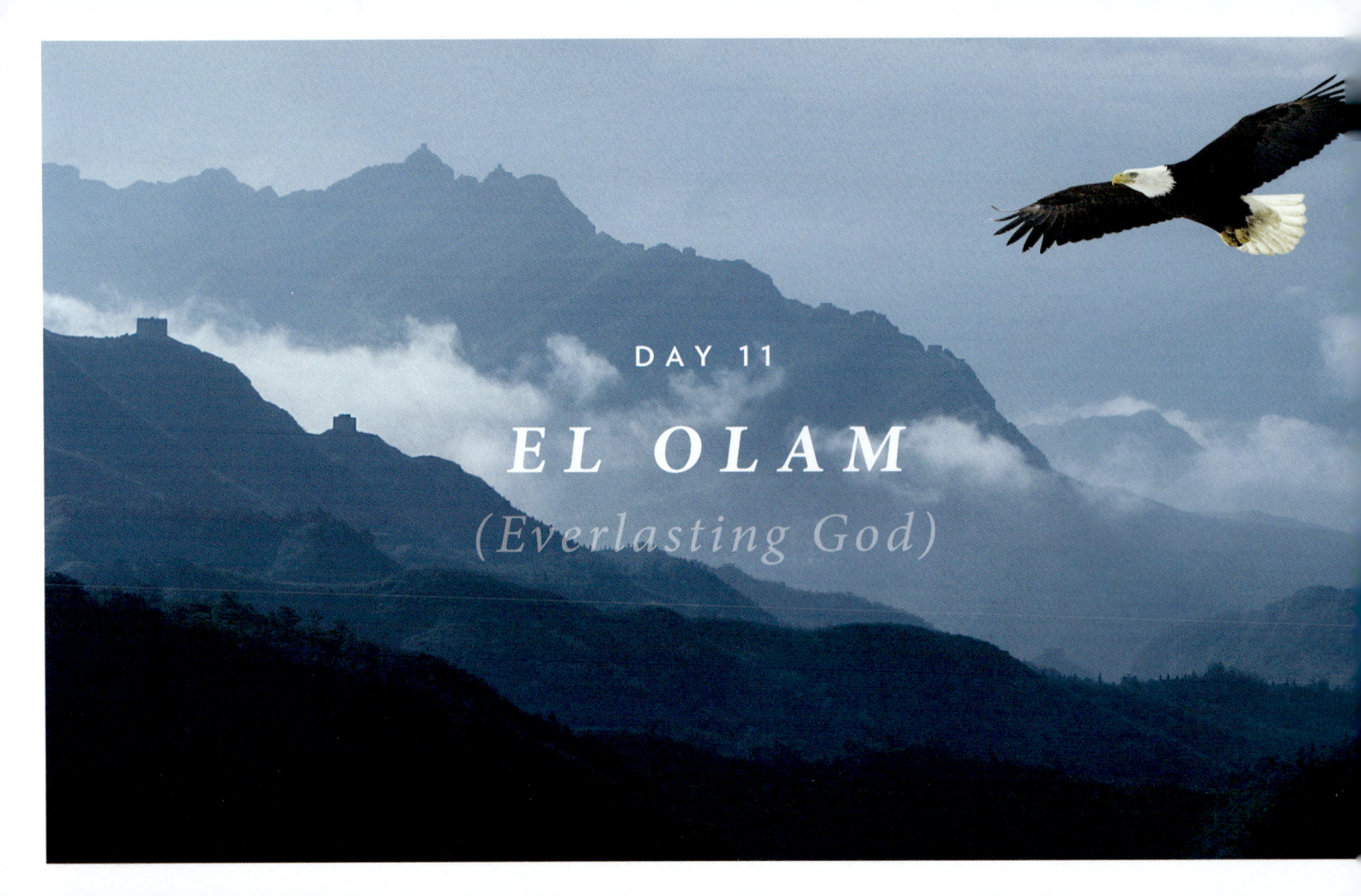

EL OLAM
(Everlasting God)

Lord, You have been our dwelling place [our refuge, our sanctuary, our stability] in all generations.

Before the mountains were born or before You had given birth to the earth and the world,

even from everlasting to everlasting, You are [the eternal] God.

PSALM 90:1-2 AMP

DAY 11

EL OLAM

From everlasting to everlasting, before the birth of the world. He is the Everlasting God — El Olam. *"I am the Alpha and the Omega, the First and the Last, the Beginning and the End"* (Revelation 22:13). He is beyond any constraints of time that the human mind can construct.

As 19th-century preacher Charles Spurgeon once wrote: "What we call past, present and future, He wraps up in one eternal NOW. And if you say that He loves you *now*, you thereby say that He loved you yesterday, He loved you in the past eternity and He will love you forever; for now with God is past, present and future."

God is not constrained by time, for . . . *with the Lord one day is as a thousand years, and a thousand years as one day* (2 Peter 3:8 NKJV). To the human mind it may seem like God has forgotten His promises (v. 9). Abraham and Sarah had to wait nearly 25 years before God fulfilled His promise to give them a child of their own. The children of Israel wandered around the desert for 40 years before entering the Promised Land. But eternal promises can be trusted when they come from an Everlasting God.

Do you not know? Have you not heard? The Lord *is the everlasting God, the Creator of the ends of the earth. He will not grow tired or weary, and his understanding no one can fathom* **(Isaiah 40:28).**

EVERLASTING GOD

How have you seen God move as the Everlasting God?

_____

_____

_____

_____

What is the Lord saying to you today about His name as EL OLAM?

_____

_____

_____

_____

DAY 12

EL ROI

(The God Who Sees Me)

And the Angel of the Lord said to her [Hagar]: "Behold, you are with child, and you shall bear a son. You shall call his name Ishmael, because the Lord has heard your affliction. He shall be a wild man; his hand shall be against every man, and every man's hand against him. And he shall dwell in the presence of all his brethren." Then she called the name of the Lord who spoke to her, You-Are-the-God-Who-Sees; for she said, "Have I also here seen Him who sees me?"

Therefore the well was called Beer Lahai Roi; observe, it is between Kadesh and Bered.

GENESIS 16:11–14 NKJV

DAY 12

EL ROI

When Sarai struggled to get pregnant, she gave Abram her Egyptian maid, Hagar. But when Hagar became pregnant, there was great animosity between the two women. Hagar fled, but the Angel of the Lord found her beside a fountain of water in the wilderness. Hagar then called God "El Roi," because He saw what she was going through and looked upon her *"[with understanding and compassion]"* (v. 13 AMP).

Nothing escapes the eye of the Father — not circumstances, not fears, not even a person's thoughts are hidden from El Roi, the God Who Sees.

Where can I go from Your Spirit? Or where can I flee from Your presence? If I ascend into heaven, You are there; if I make my bed in hell, behold, You are there. If I take the wings of the morning, and dwell in the uttermost parts of the sea, even there Your hand shall lead me, and Your right hand shall hold me **(Psalm 139:7–10 NKJV)**.

How have you seen God move as the God Who Sees You?

_____

_____

_____

_____

What is the Lord saying to you today about His name as EL ROI?

_____

_____

_____

_____

DAY 13

EL SALI

(God My Rock)

I will love You, O Lord, my strength.

The Lord is my rock and my fortress and my deliverer;

My God, my strength, in whom I will trust;

My shield and the horn of my salvation, my stronghold.

I will call upon the Lord, who is worthy to be praised;

So shall I be saved from my enemies.

PSALM 18:1-3 NKJV

DAY 13

El Sali — "God is my Rock" — is a name that describes a characteristic of God that is very prevalent in the Scriptures: God as our source of strength. In this passage, each of the descriptive phrases speaks of God's strength.

God is "my rock" and "my strength." A rock is solid, heavy and often immovable. When David said that God was his rock, he was saying that all of his success — all of his victory — wasn't in his own strength, but was due to God serving as his source of strength, the One he could always rely on to protect him and keep him safe.

God is "my fortress" and "my stronghold." A fortress is a military stronghold that protects a building from outside forces. As king, David knew the importance of a fortress to protect against attack. Looking to God as his fortress meant David was looking to God to protect him personally from not only his enemies, but also the influences of the world.

God is "my deliverer" and "my salvation," a way of escape. God regularly rescued David from the hands of his enemies, including from his predecessor King Saul.

We can do so much more in this life if we look to God as our source of strength, because *"There is no one holy like the Lord; there is no one besides you; there is no Rock like our God"* (**1 Samuel 2:2**).

GOD MY ROCK

How have you seen God move as your Rock?

___

___

___

___

What is the Lord saying to you today about His name as EL SALI?

___

___

___

___

DAY 14

EL SHADDAI

(Almighty)

Then Jacob said to Joseph: "God Almighty appeared to me at Luz in the land of Canaan and blessed me, and said to me, 'Behold, I will make you fruitful and multiply you, and I will make of you a multitude of people, and give this land to your descendants after you as an everlasting possession.'"

GENESIS 48:3–4 NKJV

DAY 14

EL SHADDAI

God appears *"to Abraham, to Isaac, and to Jacob (Israel) as God Almighty [El Shaddai]"* (Exodus 6:3 AMP). In each appearance, the Almighty confirms His covenant — His promise to multiply and make a great nation out of the sons of Abraham, Isaac and Jacob.

After El Shaddai appeared to Jacob, *Jacob made a vow, saying, "If God will be with me, and keep me in this way that I am going, and give me bread to eat and clothing to put on, so that I come back to my father's house in peace, then the* Lord *shall be my God"* (Genesis 28:20–21 NKJV).

Jacob lists his needs as: companionship, guidance, food, clothing, and safety. El Shaddai, God Almighty, is the All-Sufficient One, the One who not only pours out His blessings upon His children but also meets all their needs. Like a mother who cares for her child, so does God care for His own (Isaiah 66:13). Not one need that Jacob had went unmet.

And my God shall supply all your need according to His riches in glory by Christ Jesus **(Philippians 4:19 NKJV).**

ALMIGHTY

How have you seen God move as the Almighty?

_____

_____

_____

_____

What is the Lord saying to you today about His name as EL SHADDAI?

_____

_____

_____

_____

DAY 15

IMMANUEL

(God With Us)

"Be broken [in pieces], O peoples, and be shattered! Listen, all you [our enemies from the] far countries. Prepare yourselves [for war], and be shattered; prepare yourselves [for war], and be shattered. Take counsel together [against Judah], but it will come to nothing; speak the word, but it will not stand, for God is with us (Immanuel)."

ISAIAH 8:9-10 AMP

DAY 15

IMMANUEL

Immanuel — God with us — has brought peace to countless Christians during some of the darkest times of history, because where His presence is there is victory. In her book *The Hiding Place*, Corrie ten Boom describes how she was able to trust and serve God even in a Nazi concentration camp in the 1940s, because she felt His presence with her.

Throughout her time in the camps, Corrie had a Bible with her. Despite regular searches, showers and transfers, she was miraculously never caught with the Scriptures. God was in control of every detail, down to the bedbugs. It was the presence of those bugs that ensured that the guards would not enter the women's barracks, which gave Corrie and her sister opportunities to read the Scriptures to the other women.

Nightly Bible reading was a practice that her father had always kept in their home. Corrie remembered how, after the nightly readings, he would tuck her into bed at night as a child and place his hand upon her face, soothing her to sleep. In the concentration camps, sleep was particularly difficult for Corrie, so she would ask Immanuel to lay His fatherly hand upon her face, and sleep would come.

"Therefore the Lord Himself will give you a sign: Listen carefully, the virgin will conceive and give birth to a son, and she will call his name Immanuel (God with us)" **(Isaiah 7:14 AMP).**

How have you seen God move as always being with you?

_____

_____

_____

_____

What is the Lord saying to you today about His name as IMMANUEL?

_____

_____

_____

_____

DAY 16

JEHOVAH ELOHAY

(The Lord My God)

*For You will light my lamp; the L*ORD *my God will enlighten my darkness.*

For by You I can run against a troop, by my God I can leap over a wall.

PSALM 18:28-29 NKJV

DAY 16

When the name Jehovah Elohay is used in Scripture, it often denotes a time when the children of Israel are crying out to God for help. In Psalm 18, David is praising God for being his light in times of darkness. In Zechariah 14:5, Zechariah uses the name Jehovah Elohay when he prophesies of a day when God will come and fight against Jerusalem's enemies for them, overpowering the enemy and taking His rightful place as the One and only Ruler of all the Earth. In Matthew 27:46, when Jesus is hanging on the cross, He also cries out to Jehovah Elohay, calling on His Father to intervene: *"My God, My God, why have You forsaken Me?"*

God wants a personal relationship with all of His children; He is Jehovah Elohay — the Lord MY God. He wants His name to be the One we call on in our time of need, but that will only happen if His children see Him as a personal God — as MY God, MY Light, MY Savior, MY Redeemer, MY Defender, MY Shepherd, and MY Help in time of need. Likewise, when God looks upon you He says, "That is MY Creation." As it says in Song of Solomon 6:3, *I am my beloved's and my beloved is mine* **(NIV)**.

THE LORD MY GOD

How have you seen God move as being your God?

_____

_____

_____

_____

What is the Lord saying to you today about His name as JEHOVAH ELOHAY?

_____

_____

_____

_____

DAY 17

JEHOVAH EZER

(The Lord Our Helper)

We wait [expectantly] for the Lord; *He is our help and our shield. For in Him our heart rejoices,*

because we trust [lean on, rely on, and are confident] in His holy name.

PSALM 33:20–21 AMP

DAY 17

During the time of the kings and prophets, as described in the Old Testament, the men knew it was essential to have God on their side if they were going to win at war. If Jehovah Ezer — the Lord our Helper — was on your side, you were guaranteed victory.

In Numbers 22, Balak, king of Moab, asks Balaam to curse the Israelites so that the Moabites would have victory over them. Balak knew that the Lord's blessing was upon the Israelites and that as long as it was there, the Moabites had no chance of overtaking them.

In 1 Samuel 7, the Israelites ask Samuel to pray to God to give them victory over the Philistines. Samuel does so, and God gives them victory. *Then Samuel took a stone and set it between Mizpah and Shen, and he named it Ebenezer (stone of help), saying, "Thus far the Lord has helped us"* (v. 12 AMP).

Later, in 1 Samuel 14, after Jonathan was confident in the Lord's favor, God caused the Philistines to be confused to the point that they ended up killing their own men. Sometimes armies didn't even have to go to battle when Jehovah Ezer was around. The Lord is *our refuge and strength, always ready to help in times of trouble* (Psalm 46:1 NLT).

So we may boldly say: "The Lord is my helper; I will not fear. What can man do to me?" **(Hebrews 13:6 NKJV).**

THE LORD OUR HELPER

How have you seen God move as being your Helper?

_____

_____

_____

_____

What is the Lord saying to you today about His name as JEHOVAH EZER?

_____

_____

_____

_____

DAY 18

JEHOVAH GMOLAH

(The Lord Who Rewards)

"The Lord rewarded me according to my righteousness; according to the cleanness of my hands He has recompensed me. For I have kept the ways of the Lord, and have not wickedly departed from my God. For all His judgments were before me; and as for His statutes, I did not depart from them. I was also blameless before Him, and I kept myself from my iniquity. Therefore the Lord has recompensed me according to my righteousness, according to my cleanness in His eyes."

2 SAMUEL 22:21-25 NKJV

DAY 18

While Saul was king, David served him faithfully, both at war and in his house by playing the harp to calm him. But Saul was jealous of David because the Lord was with David and because the people sang, *"Saul has slain his thousands, and David his tens of thousands"* (1 Samuel 18:7). Saul attempted to kill David multiple times, even pursuing him when David fled for his life. But David trusted God, and he knew that God wanted him to honor Saul's position as king; so even when David had an opportunity to kill Saul, he spared his life (1 Samuel 24; 26).

After Saul's death, when David took his rightful place as king, David faced the repercussions of Saul's actions and unfair dealings with other people groups. When the nation faced a three-year famine, *David inquired of the* Lord. *And the* Lord *answered, "It is because of Saul and his bloodthirsty house, because he killed the Gibeonites"* (2 Samuel 21:1 NKJV).

When a person is treated unfairly, is wrongfully accused or has to pay for someone else's mistakes, it can be difficult to not get defensive and attack back. But from David's song in 2 Samuel 22, it is apparent that David knew his God was Jehovah Gmolah — the God of Recompense — who would reward him and exact justice on his behalf. Vengeance belongs to the Lord; retribution and recompense are His.

Do not say, "I will repay evil"; wait for the Lord, *and He will save you* (**Proverbs 20:22 NASB**).

THE LORD WHO REWARDS

How have you seen God move as a Rewarder?

_____

_____

_____

_____

What is the Lord saying to you today about His name as JEHOVAH GMOLAH?

_____

_____

_____

_____

DAY 19

JEHOVAH HOSEENU

(The Lord Our Maker)

Oh come, let us worship and bow down;

*Let us kneel before the L*ORD *our Maker.*

PSALM 95:6 NKJV

DAY 19

JEHOVAH HOSEENU

The names Elohim — God our Creator — and Jehovah Hoseenu — the Lord our Maker — go hand in hand. Elohim creates something out of nothing when He creates all things: *The earth was formless and void* (Genesis 1:2 AMP) when He created all things. And Jehovah Hoseenu takes what has already been created and molds and makes it into something beautiful: *And the Lord God formed man of the dust of the ground, and breathed into his nostrils the breath of life; and man became a living being* (Genesis 2:7 NKJV).

Another illustration is found in Jeremiah 18. God tells Jeremiah to go to the potter's house, where Jeremiah sees the potter making something at his wheel:

> *But the vessel that he was making from clay was spoiled by the potter's hand; so he made it over, reworking it and making it into another pot that seemed good to him* (v. 4 AMP).

The clay had already been created, but the potter was molding it — shaping it — into something beautiful, which often took multiple attempts to transform it into the vision that the potter had for it.

> *"O house of Israel, can I not do with you as this potter does?" says the Lord. "Look carefully, as the clay is in the potter's hand, so are you in My hand, O house of Israel"* (v. 6).

God revealed to Jeremiah that as Jehovah Hoseenu — the Lord our Maker — He was like the potter and we were like the clay, being shaped and molded into what was good in His eyes. When life becomes ugly and messy, lumpy and misshapen, you can trust in Jehovah Hoseenu, who takes what is already there and makes it into something beautiful.

THE LORD OUR MAKER

How have you seen God move as your Maker?

_____

_____

_____

_____

What is the Lord saying to you today about His name as JEHOVAH HOSEENU?

_____

_____

_____

_____

DAY 20

JEHOVAH JIREH

(The Lord Will Provide)

And Abraham lifted up his eyes, and looked, and behold behind him a ram caught in a thicket by his horns: and Abraham went and took the ram, and offered him up for a burnt offering in the stead of his son. And Abraham called the name of that place Jehovahjireh: as it is said to this day, in the mount of the Lord *it shall be seen.*

GENESIS 22:13–14 KJV

DAY 20

JEHOVAH JIREH

"*Some time later . . .*" after Sarah gave birth to Isaac, the promised child, his father Abraham was tested (Genesis 22:1). Abraham had obeyed God before Isaac was born, but had the child taken God's place in Abraham's heart? If Abraham was to become the father of many nations, God had to be sure his heart was still pure. So God told Abraham to take Isaac to Mount Moriah and sacrifice him there as an offering to the Lord.

> *Abraham took the wood for the burnt offering and placed it on his son Isaac, and he himself carried the fire and the knife. As the two of them went on together, Isaac spoke up and said to his father Abraham, "Father?" "Yes, my son?" Abraham replied. "The fire and wood are here," Isaac said, "but where is the lamb for the burnt offering?" Abraham answered, "God himself will provide the lamb for the burnt offering, my son." And the two of them went on together.* (vv. 6–8)

Jehovah Jireh — "God himself will provide the lamb." And so He did. After Isaac took his place on the altar and Abraham held the knife that would slay the boy, the Angel of the Lord spoke to Abraham from heaven, told him to not touch the boy, and said that He knew that Abraham truly feared the Lord. There in the thicket was a ram to be sacrificed in Isaac's place, not unlike the Lamb — Jesus — who would one day take the place of all humanity.

So Abraham called that place The Lord *Will Provide. And to this day it is said, "On the mountain of the Lord it will be provided"* (v. 14).

THE LORD WILL PROVIDE

How have you seen God move as your Provider?

_____

_____

_____

_____

What is the Lord saying to you today about His name as JEHOVAH JIREH?

_____

_____

_____

_____

DAY 21

JEHOVAH MAKKEH

(The Lord Who Molds Me)

"I will not look on you with pity; I will not spare you. I will repay you for your conduct and for the detestable practices among you. Then you will know that it is I the Lord who strikes you."

EZEKIEL 7:9

DAY 21

JEHOVAH MAKKEH

In Matthew 16, Jesus tells His disciples that the time has come for Him to be crucified. Peter argues with Jesus, saying he'll never let it happen. To which Jesus replies: *"Get behind Me, Satan! You are an offense to Me, for you are not mindful of the things of God, but the things of men"* (v. 23 NKJV). Jesus' rebuke seems harsh. Calling Peter "Satan"? But this is Jehovah Makkeh — the Lord who lovingly chastens, molds and corrects His children.

Solomon, the wisest man in Scripture, wrote: *My son, do not despise the LORD's discipline, and do not resent his rebuke, because the LORD disciplines those he loves, as a father the son he delights in"* (Proverbs 3:11–12).

The Lord disciplines those He loves . . . Jesus didn't discipline Peter because He was mad at him, but because He loved him. He wanted Peter to believe that God had sent Him for this purpose, and it was Peter upon whom He wanted to build His church (Matthew 16:18).

Hebrews 12:11 affirms: *No discipline seems pleasant at the time, but painful. Later on, however, it produces a harvest of righteousness and peace for those who have been trained by it.*

Peter had a rough couple of days ahead of him: days of being chastened, days of failing Jesus by denying Him, but days that would grow his faith as he learned to humble himself in total obedience to the Lord. And it was that chastening by Jehovah Makkeh that changed Simon into Peter, the rock upon whom He would build His church.

THE LORD WHO MOLDS ME

How have you seen God move as the One who molds and shapes you?

_____

_____

_____

_____

What is the Lord saying to you today about His name as JEHOVAH MAKKEH?

_____

_____

_____

_____

DAY 22

JEHOVAH MEKODDISHKEM

(The Lord Who Sanctifies You)

And the Lord *said to Moses, "But as for you, say to the Israelites, 'You shall most certainly observe My Sabbaths, for it is a sign between Me and you throughout your generations, so that you may know [without any doubt] and acknowledge that I am the* Lord *who sanctifies you and sets you apart [for Myself].'"*

EXODUS 31:12-13 AMP

DAY 22

Jehovah Mekoddishkem — "the Lord who sanctifies" — is used twice in the Old Testament. In both instances the name is used in conjunction with the Commandments of the Law, *"inscribed by the finger of God"* on tablets of stone (v. 18).

To be sanctified is to be set aside for the Lord, dedicated to Him and made holy. God was asking the children of Israel to observe the Sabbath, to set aside the day solely for Him, as an acknowledgment that He had chosen them. The children of Israel were God's chosen people — set apart from all the others — and out of them would come the Root of David — Jesus — who would bring salvation to all the world (Isaiah 11:10).

In the New Testament book of Romans, Paul writes: *Therefore I urge you, brothers and sisters, by the mercies of God, to present your bodies [dedicating all of yourselves, set apart] as a living sacrifice, holy and well-pleasing to God, which is your rational (logical, intelligent) act of worship* (12:1 AMP). How can a person be holy? Because God Himself — Jehovah Mekoddishkem — is *"the Lord, who makes you holy"* (Exodus 31:13), who sets apart, who transforms the person who could never abide by all His Commandments without Him, into a person who is "holy and well-pleasing" in His sight.

THE LORD WHO SANCTIFIES YOU

How have you seen God move as your Sanctifier?

_____

_____

_____

_____

What is the Lord saying to you today about His name as JEHOVAH MEKODDISHKEM?

_____

_____

_____

_____

DAY 23

JEHOVAH NISSI

(The Lord My Banner)

Moses said to Joshua, "Choose some of our men and go out to fight the Amalekites. Tomorrow I will stand on top of the hill with the staff of God in my hands." So Joshua fought the Amalekites as Moses had ordered, and Moses, Aaron and Hur went to the top of the hill. As long as Moses held up his hands, the Israelites were winning, but whenever he lowered his hands, the Amalekites were winning. When Moses' hands grew tired, they took a stone and put it under him and he sat on it. Aaron and Hur held his hands up — one on one side, one on the other — so that his hands remained steady till sunset. So Joshua overcame the Amalekite army with the sword. Then the Lord said to Moses, "Write this on a scroll as something to be remembered and make sure that Joshua hears it, because I will completely blot out the name of Amalek from under heaven."

Moses built an altar and called it The Lord is my Banner.

EXODUS 17:9-15

DAY 23

JEHOVAH NISSI

In Numbers chapter 1, the Lord told Moses to take a census of all the Israelites who had been rescued out of Egypt. They were divided into their family tribes (each of the twelve sons of Jacob made up its own family tribe) and assigned a specific place within the camp: *"Each tribe of Israel will camp in a designated area with its own family banner"* (v. 52 NLT).

The family banner was like a nation's flag. It indicated to whom a person or group belonged. The armies also carried banners into war, so that they would know who they were fighting for and who they were fighting against.

In Exodus chapter 17, Moses knew that the Lord had won the battle against the Amalekites, and that whoever was on the side of the Lord would always prevail. So he declared the place Jehovah Nissi — *"The Lord is my Banner."*

THE LORD MY BANNER

How have you seen God move as your Banner?

_____

_____

_____

_____

What is the Lord saying to you today about His name as JEHOVAH NISSI?

_____

_____

_____

_____

DAY 24

JEHOVAH RAAH

(The Lord My Shepherd)

The Lord is my shepherd;

I shall not want.

He makes me to lie down in green pastures;

He leads me beside the still waters.

He restores my soul;

He leads me in the paths of righteousness

For His name's sake.

Yea, though I walk through the
  valley of the shadow of death,

I will fear no evil;

For You are with me;

Your rod and Your staff, they comfort me.

You prepare a table before me
  in the presence of my enemies;

You anoint my head with oil;

My cup runs over.

Surely goodness and mercy shall follow me

All the days of my life;

And I will dwell in the house of the Lord

Forever.

PSALM 23:1–6 NKJV

DAY 24

JEHOVAH RAAH

One of God's favorite ways to describe Himself is as a Shepherd.

The relationship between the sheep (man) and the Shepherd (God) is clearly of a Master and His subjects. And yet, the Shepherd is not depicted as a typical ruler. Rather than a rod that chastens, His staff comforts (v. 4). If one sheep goes missing, He is the One who seeks him out (Ezekiel 34:11; Luke 15:4). Like David, the good Shepherd is willing to risk His life to protect His sheep (1 Samuel 17:34–35; John 10:11). And because the sheep know that the Shepherd is there to guide, protect and feed them, the sheep know His voice and willingly follow (John 10:4).

The Lord *is my Shepherd [to feed, to guide and to shield me], I shall not want* **(Psalm 23:1 AMP).**

THE LORD MY SHEPHERD

How have you seen God move as your Shepherd?

_____

_____

_____

_____

What is the Lord saying to you today about His name as JEHOVAH RAAH?

_____

_____

_____

_____

DAY 25

JEHOVAH RAPHA

(The Lord Who Heals)

"If you diligently heed the voice of the Lord your God and do what is right in His sight, give ear to His commandments and keep all His statutes, I will put none of the diseases on you which I have brought on the Egyptians. For I am the Lord who heals you."

EXODUS 15:26 NKJV

DAY 25

JEHOVAH RAPHA

Let's set the scene for Exodus chapter 15. The Israelites had just escaped captivity. They'd just seen God part the Red Sea for them, rescuing them from the hands of the Egyptians: *"The horse and its rider He has thrown into the sea!"* (v. 21). The Israelites sang praises to the Lord. But then they began to grow thirsty. Three days passed without water. When they eventually did find water, it was bitter, and so were their attitudes (vv. 23–24).

Moses cried out to the Lord for help, and the Lord responded with Exodus 15:26: I am Jehovah Rapha — *"the Lord who heals you."*

God was reminding them that He could put the same plagues on them that He put on the Egyptians — boils, locusts, death — but that He could also heal them and restore them to the good health, the good life and the faith that they once knew.

The healing that the Israelites needed at this point was as much spiritual as it was physical. While they were physically thirsty, their spiritual thirst was the one that God wanted to see quenched.

When God reminds us that He is Jehovah Rapha, He is reminding us that He can heal us: from sickness and disease, yes, because while Jesus walked the Earth, He healed the blind and the lame. But God can also heal us from sin and unrighteousness. He has provided the final cure for anything that ails us, and that is Jesus Christ.

THE LORD WHO HEALS

How have you seen God move as your Healer?

_____

_____

_____

_____

What is the Lord saying to you today about His name as JEHOVAH RAPHA?

_____

_____

_____

_____

DAY 26

JEHOVAH SABAOTH

(The Lord of Hosts)

[Hannah] was in bitterness of soul, and prayed to the Lord and wept in anguish. Then she made a vow and said, "O Lord of hosts, if You will indeed look on the affliction of Your maidservant and remember me, and not forget Your maidservant, but will give Your maidservant a male child, then I will give him to the Lord all the days of his life, and no razor shall come upon his head."

1 SAMUEL 1:10–11 NKJV

DAY 26

JEHOVAH SABAOTH

Jehovah Sabaoth — the "Lord of hosts" — is used nearly 300 times in Scripture, often to refer to God's overpowering of earthly armies. Throughout the Old Testament, Jehovah Sabaoth seems to be constantly at war, giving victory to His chosen people. The sovereignty of Jehovah Sabaoth is not only over earthly armies, however, but also over the spiritual — He is the *"Lord of Heaven's Armies"* (v. 11 NLT).

In 1 Samuel 1, Hannah calls on Jehovah Sabaoth to overpower the spiritual army that had invaded her and left her barren. Hannah's repetition of calling herself the Lord's "maidservant" in 1 Samuel chapter 1 shows that she honors the power, the sovereignty of the Lord. And He proves that sovereignty in her life, giving her a son a short time later (vv. 19–20). And as His maidservant, Hannah honored her promise to her King, dedicating her son Samuel to the Lord's service.

Who is [He then] this King of glory? The Lord of hosts, He is the King of glory [who rules over all creation with His heavenly armies]. Selah **(Psalm 24:10 AMP).**

THE LORD OF HOSTS

How have you seen God move as the Lord of Hosts?

_____

_____

_____

_____

What is the Lord saying to you today about His name as JEHOVAH SABAOTH?

_____

_____

_____

_____

DAY 27

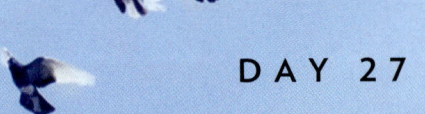

JEHOVAH SHALOM

(The Lord is Peace)

Then the Lord said to him, "Peace be with you; do not fear, you shall not die."

So Gideon built an altar there to the Lord, and called it The-Lord-Is-Peace.

To this day it is still in Ophrah of the Abiezrites.

JUDGES 6:23-24 NKJV

DAY 27

JEHOVAH SHALOM

When God told Gideon that he would save Israel, Gideon had every right to be fearful. The Israelites had been delivered into the hands of the Midianites for doing evil in the sight of the Lord for the last seven years. Despite all that God had done for them, the Israelites continued to worship other gods and were experiencing God's wrath. Not only was God not on the Israelites' side for the time being, but Gideon was both a member of the weakest clan and the weakest member of his household (v. 15). He was the weakest man of all the Israelites! What was God thinking to call him a *"mighty man of valor"* (v. 12)?

But the Lord told Gideon to have peace, that He would be with Gideon and deliver the Midianites into his hands. Gideon knew the stories of his ancestors, how God had brought them out of Egypt, and he trusted the Lord. So he built an altar to the Lord and called it "The-Lord-Is-Peace" — Jehovah Shalom.

It is interesting to note that things didn't get easier after God told Gideon to have peace; in fact, quite the opposite. Gideon had to tear down the Israelite altar of Baal — knowing that the people would protest. And then God sent him into battle with a mere 300 men. But the Lord kept His promises, and Gideon overpowered the Israelite armies.

And the peace of God, which surpasses all understanding, will guard your hearts and minds through Christ Jesus **(Philippians 4:7 NKJV)**.

THE LORD IS PEACE

How have you seen God move as your Peace?

_____

_____

_____

_____

What is the Lord saying to you today about His name as JEHOVAH SHALOM?

_____

_____

_____

_____

DAY 28

JEHOVAH SHAMMAH

(The Lord is There)

"... and the name of the city from that day shall be: The Lord Is There.*"*

EZEKIEL 48:35B NKJV

DAY 28

Jehovah Shammah — The Lord is There — not only indicates the Lord's presence but also represents a place: the New Jerusalem (Revelation 3:12). Jehovah Shammah is a reminder that no matter what has taken place in the past, or what is to come, God has not abandoned His people. There will be a restoration because the children of Israel are His, the land He created is His, there is nowhere that He isn't, and so wherever "there" is, He is.

In Ezekiel 35, God explains what happens to those who try to possess what is His:

> "Because you [descendants of Esau] have said, 'These two nations [Israel and Judah] and these two lands shall be mine, and we will take possession of them,' although **the Lord was there**, therefore, as I live," says the Lord God, "I will deal with you in accordance with the anger and envy you showed because of your hatred for them; and I will make Myself known among them [as Judge] when I judge and punish you." (vv. 10-11 AMP, emphasis added)

The Edomites would not overpower the chosen people, because **the Lord was there**.

The chapters of Ezekiel go on to discuss the restoration of Israel to God (39:25–29) and the dividing of the land according to the twelve tribes of Israel (47–48). The book ends with Jehovah Shammah: "The Lord is There."

Whether going into battle or facing daily challenges, confronting evil or looking to the future Kingdom, the name of the Lord to be called upon is Jehovah Shammah — The Lord is There.

THE LORD IS THERE

How have you seen God move as always being there?

___

___

___

___

What is the Lord saying to you today about His name as JEHOVAH SHAMMAH?

___

___

___

___

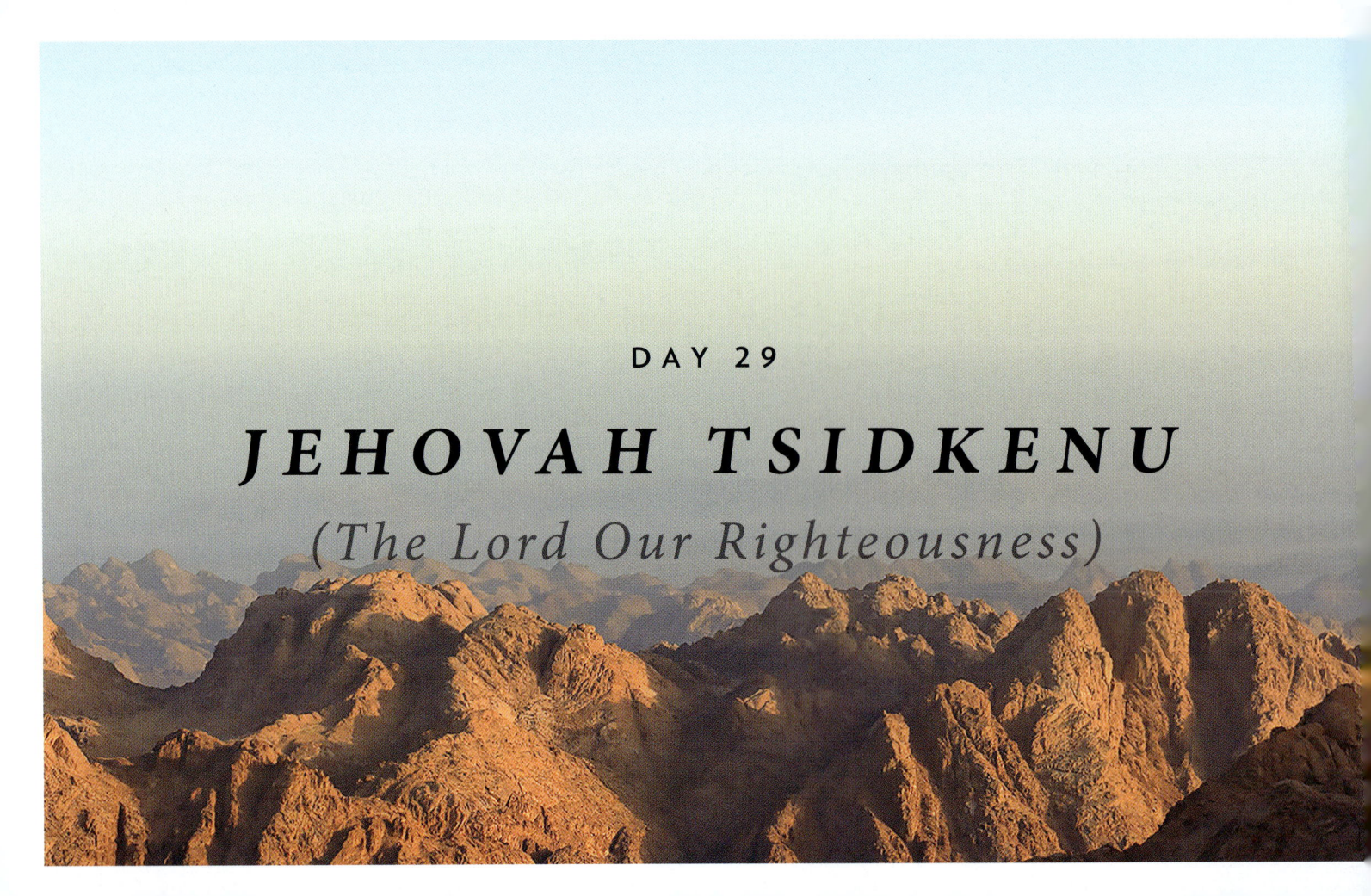

DAY 29

JEHOVAH TSIDKENU

(The Lord Our Righteousness)

"Behold, the days are coming," says the Lord, *"that I will raise to David a Branch of righteousness; a King shall reign and prosper, and execute judgment and righteousness in the earth. In His days Judah will be saved, and Israel will dwell safely; now this is His name by which He will be called:*

THE LORD OUR RIGHTEOUSNESS."

JEREMIAH 23:5-6 NKJV

DAY 29

JEHOVAH TSIDKENU

When Adam and Eve sinned in the garden of Eden, all of mankind fell from righteousness. From generation to generation that would follow, none would be without sin: *"There is none righteous, no, not one"* (Romans 3:10 NKJV). The Old Testament laws were countless, and no one was able to uphold them all. Even when God summed them up into the Ten Commandments, given to Moses on Mount Sinai (Exodus 20), the people continued to fall short.

God knew that the people would forever sin and fall short of His glory, and so He promised to send a King, from the line of David, who would reign with wisdom and do what was right in order to save the people (Jeremiah 23:5–6).

Therefore, as through one man's offense judgment came to all men, resulting in condemnation, even so through one Man's righteous act the free gift came to all men, resulting in justification of life. For as by one man's disobedience many were made sinners, so also by one Man's obedience many will be made righteous. (Romans 5:18–19 NKJV)

Without Jesus, without Jehovah Tsidkenu — The Lord Our Righteousness — none would have right standing with God. But through Him who lived a perfect life, holy and without blemish, His righteousness is imparted to all who believe.

For He made Him who knew no sin to be sin for us, that we might become the righteousness of God in Him (**2 Corinthians 5:21 NKJV**).

THE LORD OUR RIGHTEOUSNESS

How have you seen God move as your Righteousness?

_____

_____

_____

_____

What is the Lord saying to you today about His name as JEHOVAH TSIDKENU?

_____

_____

_____

_____

DAY 30

QANNA

(Jealous)

"... for you shall worship no other god, for the L{ORD}, whose name is Jealous, is a jealous God ..."

EXODUS 34:14 NKJV

DAY 30

QANNA

In the Old Testament, God frequently refers to Himself as Qanna — Jealous — when it comes to idol worship. Whether it was a golden calf constructed by Aaron (Exodus 32:4) or the household gods that Rachel hid in her camel's saddle (Genesis 31:34), God did not want to share the praise that was due only to Him with anyone else.

When God spelled out the Ten Commandments for Moses, the first four all reveal Qanna — a God who is jealous for His people's undivided devotion and honor:

> "You shall have no other gods before Me. You shall not make for yourself a carved image — any likeness of anything that is in heaven above, or that is in the earth beneath, or that is in the water under the earth; you shall not bow down to them nor serve them. For I, the Lord your God, am a jealous God, visiting the iniquity of the fathers upon the children to the third and fourth generations of those who hate Me, but showing mercy to thousands, to those who love Me and keep My commandments. You shall not take the name of the Lord your God in vain, for the Lord will not hold him guiltless who takes His name in vain. Remember the Sabbath day, to keep it holy." (Exodus 20:3–8 NKJV)

The relationship between God and Israel can be likened to a marriage in which God is a jealous husband who doesn't want His wife showing affection to anyone else.

JEALOUS

How have you seen God move as Jealous?

_____

_____

_____

_____

What is the Lord saying to you today about His name as QANNA?

_____

_____

_____

_____

DAY 31

YAHWEH

(I Am)

Then Moses said to God, "Indeed, when I come to the children of Israel and say to them, 'The God of your fathers has sent me to you,' and they say to me, 'What is His name?' what shall I say to them?" And God said to Moses, "I AM WHO I AM." And He said, "Thus you shall say to the children of Israel, 'I AM has sent me to you.'"

EXODUS 3:13-14 NKJV

DAY 31

YAHWEH

When the Lord revealed Himself to Moses in the burning bush and called him to lead the children of Israel out of Egypt, Moses was afraid the people wouldn't believe that God had sent him. "Who am I?" Moses asked. *"And who should I say has sent me?"*

Moses had given up any authority that came with his own name when he ran away from the Egyptian palace where he'd been raised, so he was looking for a name that carried weight that would therefore bestow authority on his claim. In modern times we would call this "name dropping."

"God" wasn't a significant title, because there were many gods that the people worshipped. But the personal name of the Most High God would carry weight.

God said to Moses, "I AM WHO I AM"; and He said, "You shall say this to the Israelites, 'I AM has sent me to you.'" (Exodus 3:14 AMP)

"I Am" — Yahweh, the One who is, the self-existent One. This is the personal name of God as revealed to Moses, which had never before been revealed: *"I appeared to Abraham, to Isaac, and to Jacob as El-Shaddai — 'God Almighty' — but I did not reveal my name, Yahweh, to them"* (Exodus 6:3 NLT). "Yahweh" means "to be," but also implies "to become known." God reveals Himself to Moses in an intimate way as a promise that no matter what had happened or what was to come, whether in Egypt or in the wilderness, whether in famine or in abundance, Moses could trust in the great I Am.

I AM

How have you seen God move as the great I Am?

_____

_____

_____

What is the Lord saying to you today about His name as YAHWEH?

_____

_____

_____

NOTES

NOTES

NOTES

NOTES

NOTES

NOTES

NOTES

NOTES

NOTES

NOTES

NOTES

NOTES